PAINT HORSES

by Alissa Thielges

AMICUS

pinto

foal

Look for these words and pictures as you read.

barrel

cattle

Look at that flashy horse.
It is a paint horse.

See the pinto markings?
It is a coat pattern.
It looks like white paint.

pinto

See the foal?
It is a baby horse.
It has markings, too.
It looks like its mom.

foal

Paint horses are smart.
They are quick.
They win rodeo events.

See the barrel?
A paint horse runs around it.
Well done!

barrel

See the cattle?
Paint horses work on ranches.
They help move cattle.

cattle

Paint horses are friendly.
They love treats.

pinto

See the foal?
It is a baby horse.
It has markings, too.
It looks like its mom.

foal

foal

Did you find?

barrel

See the barrel?
A paint horse runs around it.
Well done!

barrel

cattle

See the cattle?
Paint horses work on ranches.
They help move cattle.

cattle

Spot is published by Amicus
P.O. Box 227, Mankato, MN 56002
www.amicuspublishing.us

Library of Congress Cataloging-in-Publication Data
Names: Thielges, Alissa, 1995– author.
Title: Paint horses / by Alissa Thielges.
Description: Mankato, Minnesota : Amicus, [2023] | Series:
    Spot horses | Audience: Ages 4-7 | Audience: Grades
    K-1 | Summary: "Meet the Paint Horse breed in this
    leveled reader that reinforces key vocabulary with a
    search-and-find feature. Carefully controlled text and
    excellent photos introduce these smart, quick horses to
    early readers."–Provided by publisher.
Identifiers: LCCN 2021055481 (print) | LCCN 2021055482
    (ebook) | ISBN 9781645492474 (hardcover) | ISBN
    9781681527710 (paperback) | ISBN 9781645493358
    (ebook)
Subjects: LCSH: American paint horse--Juvenile literature.
Classification: LCC SF293.A47 T45 2023 (print) | LCC
    SF293.A47 (ebook) | DDC 636.1/3--dc23/eng/20211213
LC record available at https://lccn.loc.gov/2021055481
LC ebook record available at https://lccn.loc.
    gov/2021055482

Rebecca Glaser, editor
Deb Miner, series designer
Catherine Berthiaume and Grant Gould,
book design and photo research

Photos by Alamy/Barbara Jean
8-9; Getty/Tim Platt 14-15; iStock/
DaydreamsGirl 12-13; Shutterstock/skmj
cover, 16, Olga_i 1, Kwadrat 3, 4-5,
Zuzule 6-7, Diane Garcia, 10-11

PAINT HORSES